P9-ELW-210

Exploring
NEWGRANGE

LIAM MAC UISTIN

Liam Mac Uistin is an expert in celtic mythology and has long been fascinated by the stories of Irish folklore. He has won many awards for his work and is the author of numerous books.

One of his most notable awards was the selection of his prose poem, *We had a Vision,* by the Irish Government to be inscribed on a plaque in the National Garden of Remembrance in Dublin. This poem celebrates the lives of all those who have worked and died for the political and cultural freedom of Ireland.

Liam lives in Athboy, County Meath, close to the Newgrange site in the Boyne Valley.

CONSULTING EDITORS

Clare Tuffy and Craig Downie

EXPLORING
newgrange

Liam Mac Uistin

THE O'BRIEN PRESS
DUBLIN

First published 1999 by The O'Brien Press Ltd.,
12 Terenure Road East, Rathgar, Dublin 6, Ireland.
Tel. +353 1 4923333; Fax. +353 1 4922777
email: books@obrien.ie
website: www.obrien.ie
Reprinted 2001.
First published in paperback 2007.

ISBN: 978-0-86278-981-7

Copyright for text © Liam Mac Uistin
Copyright for typesetting, layout, illustrations, design
© The O'Brien Press Ltd.

All rights reserved. No part of this publication may be reproduced
or utilised in any form or by any means, electronic or mechanical,
including photocopying, recording or in any information storage and
retrieval system, without permission in writing from the publisher.

British Library Cataloguing-in-publication Data
Mac Uistin, Liam
Exploring Newgrange. - 3rd ed.
1.Megalithic monuments - Ireland - Newgrange Site 2.Tombs - Ireland - Newgrange
Site 3.Excavations (Archaeology) - Ireland - Newgrange
4.Newgrange (Ireland) - Antiquities
5. Newgrange Site (Ireland)
I.Title
936.1'822'01

3 4 5 6 7 8 9 10
07 08 09 10 11 12

The O'Brien Press receives
assistance from

Layout, editing and design: The O'Brien Press Ltd.
Drawings: Laurence Hardiman
Maps: Design Image
Printing: Graphy CEMS

Cover artefacts: front cover, top left: tri-spiral design from the chamber at Newgrange; right: entrance stone at Newgrange; left / spine: carved flint mace head from
Knowth. Back cover, left: 'beehive' quern stone; right: neolithic stone axe.

ACKNOWLEDGEMENTS
The author and publisher would like to thank the following for permission to use
photographs: Bord Fáilte 92; The National Museum of Ireland 13, 14, 16, 21; Robert
Vance 11, 77, 81, front cover and colour section,
page 1; Dúchas, The Heritage Service, all others.
The author would also like to express thanks to Richard Murphy, for
permission to use extract from his poem, 'The Cleggan Disaster',
Robert Vance, Tony Roche and Con Brogan of Dúchas, Rachel Pierce and
Íde ní Laoghaire for all their support and encouragement,
and his wife, Ailish.

This book is for Eileen

CONTENTS

Donegal

Derry

Antrim

Tyrone

Fermanagh

Armagh

Down

Monaghan

Sligo ◆ Carrowmore

Sligo ✪ Carrowkeel

Mayo

Leitrim

Cavan

Louth

Roscommon

Longford

Meath

Galway

Westmeath

Offaly

Kildare

Dublin

Laois

Wicklow

Clare

Carlow

Kilkenny

Tipperary

Limerick

Wexford

Kerry

Cork

Waterford

✪ Carrowkeel
◆ Carrowmore
◉ Dowth
⬟ Fourknocks
✳ Knowth
◼ Loughcrew
★ Newgrange

This map shows the locations of some of Ireland's most impressive
and most visited Megalithic monuments.

CHAPTER ONE

Who Built Newgrange?

Many years have passed since I first saw the great mound of
Newgrange dominating the Boyne Valley in County Meath.
It was then in a somewhat dilapidated state, overgrown in
part with nettles and other weeds. Cattle grazed around it,
unaware that they were intruding on the site of one of the
most remarkable prehistoric monuments in Europe.

Newgrange before
excavation work
began.

After some hazardous scaling of walls and fences I found
the custodian of the site, an elderly lady who lived in a nearby
cottage. Armed with a few candle stubs, and wearing a
leather apron as protection against drips of candle grease, she

escorted me to the entrance of the mound and led me inside. By the flickering candlelight the interior began to be revealed. Huge stone slabs, engraved with strange designs, loomed out of the darkness. The further I ventured along the passage the more I felt the macabre enchantment of this cold, silent, secretive place wrapping itself around me.

It is impossible to ignore the magical power of Newgrange. Once inside the tomb, I was transported back through the ages. Laying my hand on one of the beautiful spiral carvings, I could almost feel the hand of the Stone Age artist who picked out, with infinite care and precision, this mysterious communication on the silent stone. Newgrange has an undeniable sense of spiritual calm that, once experienced, is never forgotten.

When I emerged into daylight again, I was still mesmerised by the enigmatic aura of the tomb. It was some minutes before I could readjust my thoughts from images of the past to the present day.

When I revisited Newgrange in more recent times, I was fascinated by the transformation in the appearance of the tomb. The mound had been reconstructed to resemble, as closely as possible, what was considered to be its original state when completed around 3200 BC, some 5000 years ago. Seen from the valley below, with its spectacular façade of gleaming white quartz stone, Newgrange is now a striking visual reminder of its Gaelic name, Sí an Bhrú – the Fairy Mound. It has a magical appearance, like a fairy fort looming up over the valley.

Once again I ventured through the entrance and along the passage, but this time with the aid of artificial light which shows the decorative work within the tomb to its full effect. Once again I marvelled at the skill of the prehistoric people who had conceived of and constructed this astounding, lasting monument to their culture. I imagined them as ordinary people, with everyday worries and concerns, but dedicated, with unwavering determination, to the completion of this awe-inspiring project.

Newgrange as it stands today, after restoration work has replaced the white quartz façade and altered the entrance.

Who were these extraordinary people and what was their way of life? Even now, after Newgrange has been extensively excavated, relatively little is known about them. Archaeologists are still attempting to piece together their story from the sparse clues they left behind when they, and their way of life, vanished from the Boyne Valley.

WHERE DID THE BOYNE PEOPLE COME FROM?

We know from archaeological evidence that the people who built Newgrange were Neolithic or New Stone Age farmers. It is not certain where the ancestors of the Newgrange farmers originated, but they had begun to move into Ireland by about 4000 BC. It is likely that they travelled by sea from Europe, probably from Spain or Portugal.

As far as we know, the boats they sailed in were made of animal hides stretched over timber frames. It is likely that some of these currach-style craft would have been quite large and capable of carrying whole families in addition to some cows and other animals. In *Reading the Irish Landscape*, Professor Frank Mitchell estimates that boats 10m in length, with eight oarsmen and a helmsman, and with a capacity for carrying about three tonnes in weight, might have been about the ideal size to meet the challenge of a lengthy sea journey. They would also have brought various animals with them. Professor Mitchell cites Humphrey Case of the Ashmolean Museum, Oxford, who explains that each of these craft could have carried two cows and two calves, or six pigs, or ten sheep or goats, together with two dogs for herding, in addition to the human passengers. Skin bags or other water containers would also have added to the load. However, it would have been very difficult to water the animals during the voyage. As Case points out, the livestock would have posed a real danger if they became restless as they grew thirstier during the journey.

Although probably not as easy to handle as the modern currachs still in use on Ireland's Atlantic seaboard, these early boats were quite seaworthy, especially if equipped with animal skin sails in addition to oars. Nevertheless, there would have been serious risks involved in these journeys. Apart from the danger of restless animals breaking loose from their bindings and kicking a hole in the boat, there would have been the constant threat of a sudden change in the weather, the danger of fierce gales that could whip the sea into a raging frenzy:

> *'A storm began to march, the shrill wind piping*
> *And thunder exploding, while the lightning flaked*
> *In willow cascades, and the bayonets of hail*
> *flashed over craters and hillocks of water.*

(from 'The Cleggan Disaster' by Richard Murphy)

No doubt some of these boats sank before their voyage's end and their occupants were drowned.

Those who did arrive safely faced the task of starting a new life on unknown shores. Their way of life differed from that of their ancestors. Over several thousand years, farming and the domestication of animals had gradually replaced the total reliance on hunting and gathering which characterised the Mesolithic or Middle Stone Age period. (It is likely that these new techniques and ideas had spread from Asia into Europe.) When these Neolithic farmers first arrived in Ireland great

A Neolithic stone axe dating to c.3000 BC.

13

forests covered the land, like most of Europe, so the first task would have been to clear the land for fields and living space. They felled trees using axes of stone mounted on shafts of

Stone axeheads.

wood. This deforestation enabled groups to farm more land and, as agricultural methods developed, food became more plentiful and the population grew. Although this settled life meant that food was in reasonably good supply, life would still have been quite difficult and uncertain because of continuing pressures on living space and land.

WHY THE BOYNE VALLEY?

The Boyne Valley would have been a very attractive location to these New Stone Age pioneers. Like most of Ireland at that time, the valley and surrounding area would have had extensive woodlands of oak, birch and other trees. Although these people lived during what we now call the Stone Age, wood was of fundamental importance in their daily lives. Their houses, household utensils and furniture, farming equipment and so on, would all have been fashioned from wood. For example, they made a mattock or pickaxe-style implement, used to clear and cultivate the land, by mounting a flint axehead at a right angle to a hardwood shaft.

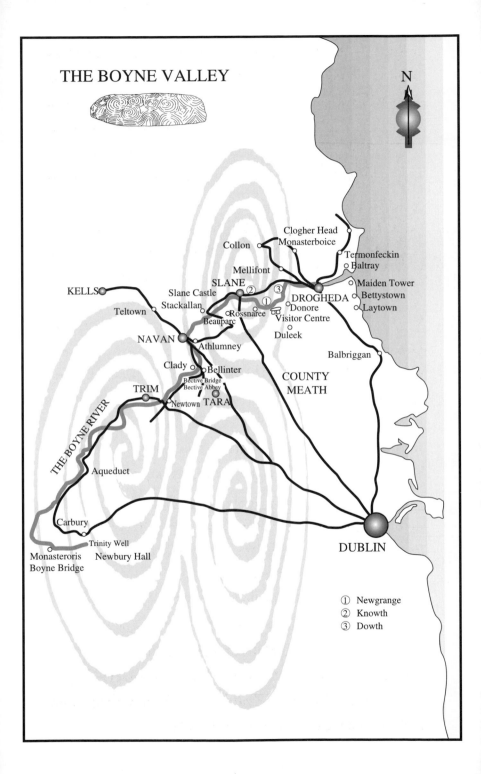

Perhaps the most important resource available in the Boyne Valley was the river Boyne itself. It provided clean drinking water and yielded an abundance of salmon and other fish. Its floodplain ensured fertile land for cultivation and grazing. It also provided access to sea-fishing as it flowed through the present-day counties of Meath and Louth and on into the Irish Sea.

The Boyne Valley provided a central location with access to many other important resources beyond its parameters. Available on the coast of Antrim were the deposits of flintstone they needed to make knives, blades and arrowheads for their yew wood longbows. With these weapons they would have hunted animals for food and defended themselves against wolves and other wild animals. The weapons would also have been used to protect their crops from hungry deer and wild boars.

Spearhead found in County Galway.

It is interesting that many of the beautifully worked and polished axeheads that have been found were clearly never intended to be used as tools. They were seen as a type of status symbol, may have had ceremonial significance and were also used as barter to trade with other communities. A fine-grained rock known as porcellanite, suitable for making these 'special' axeheads, would have been available in rea-sonably accessible areas to the north of the Boyne Valley in County Down.

Because of its strategic location and natural advantages, the people who settled there would have considered the Boyne Valley an ideal home, both on a practical as well as on a spiritual level. When they looked for a site on which to build a great monument that would dominate the landscape and be a lasting memorial to their culture, the place they chose was an elevated site where the ground rises to form a long hill commanding a panoramic view of the Boyne Valley.

The river Boyne flows for 90km before reaching the Irish Sea. Newgrange, standing on a ridge on the landscape, is visible to the right.

The burial mound of Newgrange overlooks a spectacular stretch of the river Boyne on the final stage of its journey through County Meath. Here, the river bends and loops dramatically. In doing so, it encompasses the area that was to become famous in Celtic mythology as Brú na Bóinne – the legendary burial grounds of the high kings of Tara.

The name of the river Boyne has an interesting source, steeped in ancient mythology. Traditional tales record that the river was named after Boann, a Celtic water-goddess and wife of Nechtan, a water-god. According to legend, Boann approached the well of Segais, which was reputed to be the source of all knowledge. Only four people were permitted to go there: her husband, Nechtan, and his three cupbearers or *cornairi ór*. Boann ignored this directive and to show her contempt she walked around the well anticlockwise, a gesture which defied the rules of ancient magic. The waters of the well immediately rose up to engulf her, and when she tried to escape the waters pursued her and she drowned. The course of the waters' pursuit of Boann formed the course of the river Boyne.

THE BOYNE SETTLERS

Before the arrival of the Neolithic farmers, Ireland was sparsely populated by small roving bands of hunter-gatherers. Archaeologists refer to the lifestyle and the types of stone tools these people left behind as Mesolithic or Middle Stone Age. In Ireland, the Mesolithic period lasted from roughly 7500–4500 BC. The Boyne settlers, however, were a Neolithic community. The Neolithic period, or New Stone Age, was characterised by important advances in human development. Neolithic societies produced superior tools to those of their forebears. They also made pottery, they domesticated animals and, most importantly, they practised agriculture.

A domestic scene in the Boyne settlement. The women prepare food, crushing grains in a saddle quern, while the men set out hunting with longbows of yew and quivers of deerskin.

The advance of agricultural methods led directly to permanent settlements. Unlike their Early and Middle Stone Age ancestors, the people of the Boyne Valley would not have been forced to move and resettle according to the seasons. Because they could cultivate the land year round, they could settle as a proper community. This also meant that they could plan to build their massive monuments because the community would remain in place to finish the work and to honour the dead. It is largely thanks to the advent of agriculture that we have these extraordinary monuments to Stone Age culture in Europe. For these reasons, the Neolithic period is considered by many archaeologists to be the most important era of evolution in the history of humanity.

Despite the vast amount of archaeological research and excavation at the Neolithic sites of the Boyne Valley, it is still difficult for archaeologists to be certain about details of the daily lives of the Boyne settlers. Time has whittled down the remnants of their lives, leaving only sparse clues for us to try to decipher.

As few remains of Neolithic houses have been found in the Boyne Valley, we are forced to rely on educated guesswork to

THE AGES OF THE STONE AGE

European history is divided into three distinct ages: the Stone Age, the Bronze Age and the Iron Age. The Stone Age is further divided into three periods: the Palaeolithic, the Mesolithic and the Neolithic. The Palaeolithic was the longest of these periods, stretching across 2.5 million years. It is characterised by the use of simple, chipped stone tools. The Mesolithic period was the middle period of the Stone Age, a transitional period between the Early and Late Stone Age. Finally, the Neolithic period, which directly preceded the Bronze Age, lasted from c.6000 BC until c.3000 BC.

establish what kind of domestic structures were built. The Visitor Centre at Brú na Bóinne displays a reconstruction of what is considered to be a typical Neolithic dwelling. It is a round house, thatched with rushes from the river, with walls of wattle and daub. There would have been a hearth at the centre of the house where a fire was kept burning for warmth and cooking. The people likely slept on beds of animal skins made comfortable and soft with straw and rushes. For the safety of the community, these houses were probably arranged in clusters. They probably built the stockades for their animals close to their houses so that they could keep the animals safe from unwelcome intruders such as hungry wolves.

We do not know if these early Irish farmers had sheep, but we know they did not have horses or chickens, although pig and dog bones have been discovered. They did not grow vegetables like potatoes and carrots but were limited to cereal crops – the main crops grown were wheat and barley. Their agricultural methods would have been basic and farming would have been very hard work. To prepare the land they would have used simple wooden ploughs pulled by oxen. Cattle were

'Beehive' quern stone dating to the first century AD.

raised, probably as much for their hides as for their milk and meat.

Flint was a highly-prized material in early societies. It was indispensable for the production of the many knives and blades that would have been used for cutting up animal meat, preparing hides, working wood and so on. While farming was the main source of food, additional elements from the wild would have varied the diet and helped to supplement the food stock in periods of shortage. The river Boyne would have provided salmon and other fish as well as other resources. Also, the area's wide range of plants would have been used for many purposes.

The domestic chores would probably have been performed mainly by the women. In order to make flour for cooking they would have used saddle querns. A saddle quern was a very simple type of hand mill. It consisted of a hollow stone into which the grain was placed. A round stone was then pushed backward and forward over the pile of grain in the hollow to crush it.

Hunting would also have been a task for the community. Long bows made of yew would have been used to wound and kill prey. The arrows they used were probably made of hazel wood tipped with flint points. These would have been carried in quivers made of deerskin.

Although evidence for the type of clothing they wore is sparse, some details can be gleaned indirectly. For example, round-shaped scrapers were found during excavation. These would have been used to scrape animal skins clean, suggesting the making of leather garments. Some clothes were probably woven from materials such as flax, nettles, grass and tree fibres. It is likely that cloaks woven from grass were also worn, while shawls could have been made from knotted dog hair. It is possible that dog and human hair were used to sew pieces of leather together. Tunics were probably made from animal fur and leather, while trousers, which were worn under tunics, and shoes would also have been made of leather. The bone and antler pins found among cremated remains indicate that these items were used as fasteners on garments and in the hair.

WHY WAS NEWGRANGE BUILT?

The Boyne settlers' reason, or reasons, for building Newgrange can now only be a matter of speculation. Nonetheless, the shape and features of the monument, as well as the fragments of cremated human remains found inside the chamber, indicate that its primary purpose was to serve as a burial place. This theory is supported by the fact that the hill on which it is built had already been selected as a sacred place a long time before the monument was conceived. There had been an earthen mound on the site for several hundred years. This suggests that the hill had a special spiritual significance for the Neolithic people, a significance which they wished to bestow on their deceased relatives.

Newgrange and its sister tombs at Knowth and Dowth were all part of the Megalithic tomb tradition of the Neolithic period. The word 'megalith' means 'large stone' and denotes their use in the building of these massive monuments. The Megalithic tomb tradition spread across western Europe, with the earliest tombs being built in Brittany in France around 4000 BC.

While it is generally accepted that the Megalithic structures of the Boyne Valley were intended to serve as burial places, archaeologists now feel that the tombs, as part of the new, settled life of the Neolithic period, could have served several purposes. It is thought that they were used not only as burial places but also as focal points for the wider community and as territorial markers—defining the land owned and worked by a particular group. Monuments like Newgrange also proclaimed the power and wealth of the living as well as the presence of the spirits of the ancestors. Regardless of its many possible functions, there was certainly a strong religious or spiritual motive behind the building of the monument.

WHAT'S IN A NAME?

The Irish name for Newgrange is Sí An Bhrú, the Fairy Mound of Brú an Bóinne. It is also known as Sí Aonghusa, or the Fairy Mound of Aonghus. According to Celtic legend, Aonghus, the Celtic God of Light was supposed to live at Newgrange. The modern name of Newgrange dates from the Middle Ages when the land surrounding the monument was granted to the Cistercian monastery of Mellifont as one of its granges or outlying farms. Grange is a very common place-name element in the area. Across the river from Newgrange is the townland of Roughgrange, while just beside it is Littlegrange and Sheepgrange. So Newgrange is not just the name of the monument but also of the townland surrounding it.

As relatively few bones were recovered from inside Newgrange, some experts say that this proves that the people whose remains were placed in the chamber were in some way special or revered in the community — perhaps the wisemen and wisewomen, healers, storytellers or astronomers.

On the same basis, there has been much speculation that the tomb was intended as a royal burial site, providing a final resting place for kings or chieftains and their families. However, this cannot be verified as there is no definitive evidence of exclusive royal usage, such as that found in the royal tombs of ancient Egypt and other countries. The only arguably royal or prestige objects have been found at Knowth: one is a remarkable carved mace head made of flint, the other is a great stone basin with elaborate carvings, the artistry of which far exceeds that found on the stone basins in Newgrange. For some archaeologists these objects refuel the debate and lend credence to the belief that Newgrange, Knowth and Dowth were indeed royal burial sites.

Whatever the speculation, the fact is that we know very little about the people whose bones were found inside Newgrange and nothing about their social system, language or religion. The stories their bones tell are of the person's aches, pains and approximate age at death, but nothing more.

Nowadays, many experts are of the opinion that the tombs were continually reused and that the remains of the dead were removed after a certain length of time and replaced by the recently deceased. Others suggest that if Professor O'Kelly found so many bones after 260 years of damage caused by visitors, then originally there must have been the bones of hundreds of people in the tomb. In *Reading the Irish*

Landscape, this line of thought is explored by Professor Mitchell. He speculates that perhaps Newgrange and its sister tombs at Knowth and Dowth were once filled with masses of cremated bone, as was the case at the nearby royal site of Tara. (During excavations at the Mound of the Hostages at Tara, this passage grave was found to be packed with a large quantity of cremated human bone derived, perhaps, from as many as two hundred bodies.)

BRÚ NA BÓINNE

Literally translated as 'Mansion or Palace of the Boyne', Brú na Bóinne is the collective name for the three great tombs in the Boyne Valley: Newgrange, Knowth and Dowth. According to Celtic legend, the burial mounds were the homes of gods of the underworld. Aonghus, the god of love, is supposed to have made Newgrange his home and turned it into a wonderful place where fruit trees were always laden with a heavy burden of perfectly ripe fruit.

Whether the tomb was intended for the chosen few or for the whole community, archaeologists generally agree that the Boyne settlers did believe in some form of afterlife. However, we will never know what form of other world they imagined, hoped for or feared. There were no tools or weapons found inside Newgrange, so perhaps the farmers hoped for a new life in the other world, a life without work or fighting.

It is thought that the settlers related their religious beliefs to the cycle of the seasons. They watched and measured the sun's yearly journey and saw that even this mighty globe lost its strength and life-giving power during winter. Perhaps they related the sun's cycle to their own lives and hoped that, just as winter was followed by spring, new life followed death. Because of the importance of the sun in their way of life, especially as a symbol of renewal and regeneration, it is generally believed that these people may have worshipped the sun as a deity. Many believe that it was in order to honour the sun that they built their enduring monument in the Boyne Valley.

It is very common for ancient monuments to be carefully aligned to solar, lunar or even stellar events. At other prehistoric sites, such as Stonehenge in England, the ancient people constructed monuments so that they are oriented towards the place on the horizon where the sun rises on the longest day of the year: Midsummer Day. This occurs when the sun is at its strongest, around 21 June every year. At Newgrange, however, the orientation is designed to allow the sun's rays to enter the tomb on the mornings around 21 December, the date of the winter solstice which marks the shortest day of the year in the Northern Hemisphere.

For the Boyne community, this annual occurrence surely had great celebratory significance. The passage of the sun's warm light into the chamber on the morning of the winter solstice marked the continuing of the cycle of the seasons and the safe 'rebirth' of the sun after the dark days of winter. It may also have symbolised a renewal of life in some other world for their deceased relatives. An alternative theory suggests that perhaps the Boyne people believed that the spirits of their ancestors travelled back along the beam of light as it departed from the chamber and were rejuvenated by the sun. In building this spectacular monument to house the remains of the dead, and in giving this monument the unique power of 'capturing' the sun's rays, they were perhaps endeavouring to create a physical link between death and life, a link which may indeed have been their primary motive in constructing Newgrange.

Of course, there must have been some doubt in the people's minds as to whether or not their hopes for this great monument would indeed be fulfilled. Once the mound had been completed, the Boyne people would have had to wait until the next winter solstice to see if the passage would light up, if the sun would indeed pierce the chamber and bestow its warmth on the cold darkness within. Let us imagine the scene on that eventful morning.

NEWGRANGE AND THE FIRST WINTER SOLSTICE

Before sunrise the people have gathered outside and inside the tomb. Many of them would not have been born when the building work commenced many years before. Others would have died during the long period of the monument's construction, their ashes lying in the recesses off the chamber with those of their ancestors.

The people shiver in the cold morning air as they wait for the sun to rise. A murmur of excitement ripples through those outside as the first light of dawn begins to show in the southeastern sky. The light grows slowly and the stars disappear from view. Then the great orange globe of the sun emerges over the horizon. Suddenly, gleaming rays of light shine through the roof-box, giving the passage and chamber a golden hue. The light gradually grows and the people gathered inside feel the reviving glow of the sun. They shout with joy. The people outside take up the shout that echoes across the valley. The sun now rises higher in the sky, bathing the monument in its light.

After a while, the crowd slowly disperses and the people return to their homes, happy in the knowledge that from now on the days will grow longer and warmer and life will flourish once more.

CHAPTER TWO

A Closer Look at Newgrange

HOW WAS NEWGRANGE CONSTRUCTED?

The construction of Newgrange would have required a considerable amount of planning over many years. In 3200 BC, the Boyne Valley was home to a wealthy and sophisticated society. To honour and elevate the ancestors who had chosen such a blessed place to live, the community decided to build an everlasting monument to their dead – a monument that would also mark their own prosperity and skill. The Boyne people must have realised how daunting their task would be. It would have involved careful organisation and a large, committed labour force. How was this undertaking accomplished?

In *Reading the Irish Landscape*, Professor Mitchell speculates that out of a local population of 1200 persons, a work force of about 400 could have been available to undertake the building work. He estimates that during the two-month lull in farm operations each spring, a work force of this size could have been mobilised for such tasks as clearing the site, carrying earth and other materials, quarrying and dressing stones and transporting them to the site. The labourers worked without the benefit of wheeled transport and the work would have been dangerous and exhausting. Once committed to the project, it may have taken the population of the area many years, perhaps generations, to complete their monument.

Although the pyramids of Egypt were built more than 1000 years later, the organisational problems facing the Newgrange builders would have been somewhat similar. Most experts would agree with Professor Mitchell's suggestion that there must have been an overall authority or overlord to direct the work and social organisation involved. All members of the community would have been involved in some way during the busy periods of construction. The many labourers needed to be organised and fed, this would have required engineers, surveyors, artists, ropemakers, animal handlers, carpenters, cooks, all answerable to supervisors who ensured that they worked as an efficient team.

Before a single stone could be laid, however, the architects had to ensure that the inner chamber of the monument would receive the rays of the rising sun on the morning of the winter solstice. How did they achieve this feat of engineering and mathematical calculation with only the most basic of tools to aid them?

Early farming societies were careful observers of nature and the changing of the seasons. Before calendars and before clocks, the annual course of the sun's journey in the sky was more keenly observed than it is today. The Boyne community's astronomers and architects would have assembled on the hill over many years, plotting and observing the sun, moon and stars in their mysterious but deliberate journeys across the sky. They would have placed wooden posts in the ground to help survey and record the route of the sun's rays as it rose and set each day throughout the year, moving southwards across the horizon. By placing and adjusting these markers, they would have had a clear, physical line, or alignment, marking the precise point of the sun's rising on the winter solstice. This would have provided a guide as to how the monument should be built so that the rays of the sun would penetrate the passage and reach the central chamber before fading away again.

When the sky-watchers and architects had completed their calculations and plans, the builders would have been ready to take over and start the actual construction work. However, first they had to find the types of stone required and devise a means of transporting the stones, many of them large and heavy, back to the Boyne Valley and up to the site on the hill.

THE STONES OF NEWGRANGE

Most of the large stones, the 'building blocks' of the monu- ment, are a coarse sandstone known as greywacke. The bulk of the mound is made up of smaller stones collected from the river terraces just below the site where the builders were working. The front is faced with white quartz and small, dark, water-rolled granite stones. Professor Michael J. O'Kelly, the archaeologist who excavated Newgrange

The transportation of boulders up to the site of the monument above the Boyne Valley.

between 1962 and 1975, claimed that all of the large slabs were weathered boulders. This means that they were not quarried and brought from a single source. The builders had searched for and collected these stones from a wide area. Some were found and retrieved from the Boyne riverbed and others were found lying on the surface. None of the stones was split or shaped.

Once located, the huge slabs had to be handled and prepared for their journey to the chosen site using only stone tools, wood and ropes braided from plant and animal fibres. About 450 of these large stones were used in building the structure. The largest stone is more than 4m in length and probably weighs several tonnes. All of the stones weigh more than one tonne.

There is no definite evidence to reveal how exactly the Boyne people managed to move these boulders across land for many miles. Perhaps they were transported by boat downriver to the site. Perhaps teams of oxen were employed to pull them, we simply do not know for sure. However, the most likely explanation is that, with the aid of heavy wooden levers, they placed the boulders on a line of felled tree trunks, creating a conveyor belt of sorts. The boulders could then be hauled up the hill and levered into position. The only certainty is that these Stone Age people were innovative problem solvers. But it remains one of the great mysteries of the monument, as it is with other ancient Megalithic structures, just how they managed to move and position these massive stones.

Making the enormous covering mound at Newgrange also required a remarkable amount of organisation and dedication. Newgrange is mostly made up of smaller, hand-sized stones. These were taken from the river terraces and probably carried up the hill in baskets or sacks on labourers' backs. It is estimated that some 200,000 tonnes of these stones were used. It is a twenty-minute climb from the river to the monument and many hundreds of people would have worked at this backbreaking task. It is an astonishing achievement.

The last and perhaps most valued construction materials needed were the quartz and granite stones used to create the imposing white façade. A good deal of effort was put in to finding these stones. The quartz came from County Wicklow, about 80km to the south, and the rounded granite stones were collected from the north shore of Dundalk Bay, about 50km to the north.

THE STRUCTURE OF NEWGRANGE

Megalithic tombs in Ireland fall into one of four categories: court tombs, wedge tombs, portal tombs and passage tombs. The major Boyne monuments, Newgrange, Knowth and Dowth, are passage tombs. Passage tombs also occur in other western European countries but the Irish models are the largest. There are at least 250 recorded examples of this type in Ireland. Like the other types of Megalithic structures, passage tombs are defined by their design and layout. They all have a passage made of large stones leading to a central,

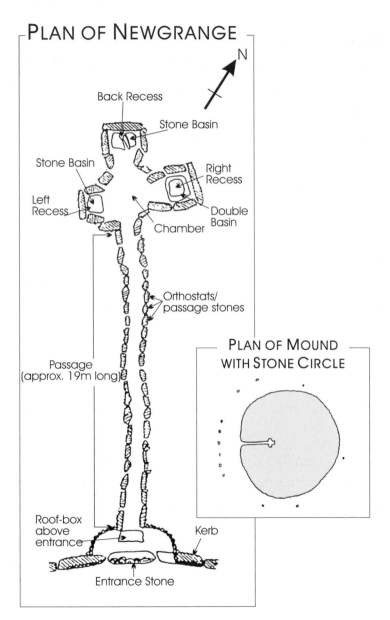

PLAN OF NEWGRANGE

N

Back Recess

Stone Basin

Stone Basin

Right Recess

Left Recess

Double Basin

Chamber

Orthostats/ passage stones

PLAN OF MOUND WITH STONE CIRCLE

Passage (approx. 19m long)

Roof-box above entrance

Kerb

Entrance Stone

roofed chamber. The passages vary in length and the chambers vary in shape and size. Usually, the chambers are round with recesses or side chambers. In Ireland, the most common interior arrangement is for the structure to have three side recesses, giving the chamber a cruciform shape. The passage and chamber are covered over either by a mound of stones (a cairn), a mound of earth (a barrow), or by a carefully layered mixture of both.

The Irish passage tomb tradition and the religious ideology that stimulated it did not originate in Ireland. Long before Newgrange was completed, similar passage tombs were being built at Gavrinis and other parts of Brittany. However, it is in the Boyne Valley that the skills of Stone Age architects and artists reached the peak of their expression. The evidence accumulated by archaeologists over the years suggests the Neolithic Brú na Bóinne complex was probably the most important cultural centre in Europe at that time.

THE EXTERIOR

The Mound

The mound at Newgrange was originally drum-shaped – it had a flat top and steep sides. It is now about 12m high, about 80m across and totally dominates the landscape, just as it did 5000 years ago.

Over the years the sides fell forward, giving the mound a more rounded, natural looking shape. The quartz and granite of the original façade lay at the bottom of the collapsed material. Following excavation, Professor O'Kelly decided to restore the front part of the mound to its original appearance. He was able to tell the height and angle of the original retaining wall by analysing the way the mound's walls had slipped

37

forward. Nowadays, as a result of his work, the mound of Newgrange looks much as it did on the day it was completed.

Within the mound, the Neolithic builders incorporated sods from their fields. They needed these sods to stabilise the tonnes of loose stones. Archaeologists have analysed the pollen and seeds in these sods and are able to tell us the types of plants, trees and grasses which were growing at that time.

The Kerb

The base of the mound is held in place by 97 huge greywacke kerbstones. When the loose stones of the mound collapsed, the kerb stayed in place, holding the original shape of the monument against the pressure of the collapsing materials. Many of these kerbstones are wonderfully carved with elaborate patterns and motifs. There are spirals, lozenges, arcs,

The magnificently carved entrance stone at Newgrange.

circles, cup marks and all types of coils and swirls. There are no obvious representations of people, animals, plants or identifiable objects. The art is entirely abstract and yet the stones display a dramatic sense of composition and a deep sense of meaning.

The best known kerbstone is the entrance stone or Kerbstone 1 (K1). Its perfectly carved spiral designs are world famous and are justly regarded as one of the finest achieve-

Kerbstone 52 (K52) at the back of the mound.

ments of European prehistoric art. The only other stone to rival it is also at Newgrange. This stone, Kerbstone 52 (K52), is at the back of the mound, diagonally opposite the entrance stone. K52 is a wonderful piece of art and more than any other stone at Newgrange is considered true sculpture. The artist let the contours of the stone suggest the designs rather than trying to impose a pattern on it.

In the past, visitors to the monument and experts alike believed that there would be another passage behind K52. Professor O'Kelly's excavations failed to uncover any more passages, but what he did discover was in many ways more exciting. He found evidence to suggest that before Newgrange was built there was already an earthen mound on the hill and that the edge of this earlier mound corresponded with the edge of Newgrange at the point where K52 was later placed. Many believe that in giving this wonderful stone such special treatment the artists and architects were honouring the builders of the earlier mound.

When we think of art nowadays we suppose that it is created with the intention of being displayed. However, at Newgrange the art on many of the stones continues beyond the visible surfaces. During the excavations it was found that many of the stones were carved on their undersides and on the sides that are turned inwards towards the cairn. Whatever the art meant to the builders of these enigmatic monuments, perhaps it was not necessarily intended to be seen by the living. On the other hand, it is also possible that the builders reused stones that had been part of earlier monuments.

The exact meaning of the abstract symbols on the kerbstones has defied all efforts at interpretation. The most popular theory is that the forms represent the changing seasons – the passage tomb builders' preoccupation with time and with marking major solar events like the solstices and the equinoxes.

Other examples of characteristic passage tomb art such as this are found in tombs at Loughcrew and Fourknocks, both

Kerbstone 67 (K67) is decorated with spiral and lozenge designs.

in County Meath. While there do not appear to be any precise parallels with art in similar tombs in Brittany, Spain and Portugal, some theories suggest that these continental counterparts might possibly have been sources of inspiration for the Irish tomb-artists.

THE INTERIOR

The Passage

The entrance to the tomb faces southeast. Today, visitors to the monument use modern wooden steps to get over the kerbstones, but in the Stone Age those who were entering the narrow passage had to climb over the entrance stone. This is about a metre high and presents a considerable physical barrier. More importantly, it probably represented a psychological barrier to those who held Newgrange sacred. It may have been seen as the threshold of the other world, the point where the world of the dead met the world of the living.

The passage is lined with large stones (orthostats) and is 19m long.

Above the entrance to the passage is a small rectangular opening known as the roof-box. It is this ingenious feature that enables the sunlight to penetrate the chamber at dawn on the winter solstice. There is a large slab just to the right of the entrance which would have been the door that sealed the tomb 5000 years ago. The roof-box was also blocked some time in the past with large pieces of white quartz.

The passage is lined on each side with large standing stones or orthostats. It is narrow and low in places but today's visitors have the benefit of electric lights to guide them. Long ago, people made their way up the passage by the flickering light of a naked flame which must have been a claustrophobic and frightening experience. About halfway up the passage there is a slight bend to the right and after this point one can no longer see back to the entrance and daylight. The passage is only about 19m long, but as one enters the chamber it feels so cold, still and quiet that the outside seems a world away.

The Chamber

The chamber has needed very little conservation and no restoration. It stands today exactly as it did all those thousands of years ago. It is a small room in comparison to the size of the covering mound and has three side chambers or recesses leading off it. It is made of large slabs of rock – those that make up the walls of the chamber standing upright, and those making the roof lying horizontally. Between the large rocks, the builders jammed smaller rocks to fill the gaps.

Some of the slabs are beautifully carved and others are plain. It is hard to imagine what kind of ceremonies took place there 5000 years ago, but even today, long after the Stone Age people who built it are gone, the chamber still has an aura of calm and peace.

The chamber has been accessible since 1699 and, unfortunately, many of the earlier visitors to the monument damaged it. Digging caused the most serious damage, but many people carved their names on the walls. Nowadays, laws protect all of the monuments; as we learn more about them and the people who built them, we treat them with greater respect.

The celebrated corbelled chamber roof
is considered one of the finest existing examples
from Stone Age Europe.

The Chamber Roof

The most astonishing feature of the chamber is the roof. It is corbelled, meaning that it is dome-shaped and made with large, interlaced slabs of rock. Each large stone slightly overlaps the one below it, until eventually the gap at the top becomes so narrow that it can be capped with one massive capstone. The sophistication of the chamber roof indicates that the builders had a great deal of experience in vault building by the time they came to build the roof at Newgrange. Indeed, this roof was so well built that it has remained watertight for 5000 years – enough to make any modern builder envious!

All of the corbels slope slightly downwards so that any water that seeps through the large mound is directed away from the interior. The builders also carved gutters onto the upper side of the roof stones covering the passage so that the water would not leak through there. To make certain that no water got in, the builders concocted a mixture of burnt clay and sea sand and packed this between the stones to seal all the spaces. It is a great stroke of luck that they took this extra precaution. Analysing this burnt clay material using radiocarbon dating techniques, archaeologists were able to confirm the monument's age.

The Recesses

The chamber has three recesses. The one on the right as one enters is the largest. On the floor of this recess are two stone basins, whereas the left and back recesses have only one basin. The stone basin in the back recess is broken and the story goes that it was broken in 1795 by a man from Connaught who had a dream that there was gold buried there.

The right recess and the unusual double basin.

He was in such a rush to get the gold after coming halfway across the country to claim it, he broke the stone basin to dig underneath it!

The upper basin in the right-hand recess is a wonderful piece of work. It has been shaped from granite, which is a very hard stone to carve. The granite basin sits on top of a large slate stone, which seems much plainer and duller by comparison. Yet, it is thought that it may be the more significant stone of the two. When you look closely, you can see that

Roofstone of the right recess.

this stone is too big to have been brought into the chamber *after* it was built. Some experts believe that for the Stone Age people this was the holiest stone in the building. They imagine that this stone was on the hill for a long time before Newgrange was built. Perhaps it was placed there by the first people to settle in the Boyne Valley and as such was particularly revered.

A cremation ritual outside the tomb. In the background, cremated remains are carried into the chamber to be deposited in the stone basins. The façade of the tomb is a modern reconstruction but is believed to be faithful to the original appearance of the monument.

The back recess at Newgrange.

On the wall in the back recess is the tri-spiral, a complicated swirl of three connecting spirals which is probably the
best known motif of Newgrange and of the Stone Age.

The broken basin in the back recess and the one on the floor
of the left recess are both made of sandstone. It is believed
that all of the basins held the remains of the dead. Generally
the burial rite consisted of cremation, but some unburnt
bones have also been found. During excavation in the 1960s,

Professor O'Kelly recovered the remains of five individuals. Three of them had been cremated. Accompanying these human bones were pendants, beads, pins and other typical grave goods made of clay and bone. These might have been funeral offerings to the gods, or intended to accompany the dead on their journey into another world.

The left recess with stone basin and large spiral designs.

CHAPTER THREE

A Megalithic Trinity

A LOOK AT KNOWTH AND DOWTH

Knowth

Knowth kept its many secrets and its long and complicated story hidden until quite recently. In 1849, Sir William Wilde recorded that 'as far as we can judge by external appearances...it appears to be as yet uninvestigated; but as there are no means of access to its interior we can only speculate as to its use'. We now know that Knowth is a more complex structure than Newgrange.

Knowth under excavation.

The great complex at Knowth comprises a central mound surrounded by 18 smaller satellite tombs. The large mound covers two distinct passage tombs, opening from the eastern and western sides respectively, and therefore referred to as Knowth East and Knowth West. The two passages lay hidden for many centuries but were rediscovered separately in 1967 and in 1968.

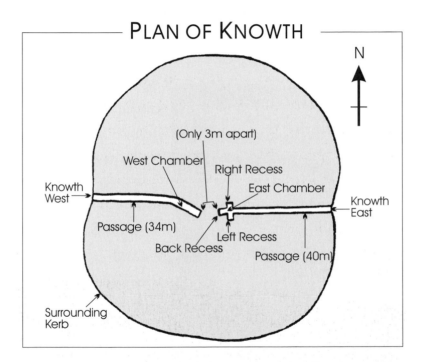

PLAN OF KNOWTH

N

(Only 3m apart)

West Chamber

Right Recess

East Chamber

Knowth West →

Knowth East

Passage (34m)

Left Recess

Back Recess

Passage (40m)

Surrounding Kerb

The west passage is about 34m long while the east passage is about 40m (the passage at Newgrange is 19m long). Each passage leads to its own central chamber and these chambers are only a few metres apart, nearly back to back under the great mound.

The entrance stone at the western side has rectangular carvings and a vertical line running down its face, like the entrance stone at Newgrange. The passage stones in Knowth West are also finely decorated and the chamber at the end of this passage is square and flat-roofed. It is less striking than the chamber on the eastern side, which is a magnificent example of Megalithic architecture.

Knowth East differs from its west-facing counterpart in that its chamber has three recesses and is cruciform. The chamber has a corbelled roof. The stone basin occupying the

The beautiful stone basin in Knowth East.

right-hand recess has curved designs, these designs are repeated on the passage stones.

As the tombs are facing due east and due west respectively, it follows that they were built to catch the rays of the rising and setting sun at the equinoxes. The equinox is the date on which the sun crosses the equator and consequently day and night are of equal length. This phenomenon occurs biannually. This means that twice a year, at the Vernal (21 March) and Autumnal (21 September) equinoxes, the Stone Age people would have gathered at

Knowth just as they gathered at Newgrange and at Dowth for the winter solstice.

Knowth remained a centre of considerable importance until the end of the Middle Ages. Whereas its initial and primary role during the Neolithic period was ceremonial and religious, the site continued to be used by various cultures and for different purposes over several thousands of years. In the Early Bronze Age (about 2000 BC), the site was used for burial and habitation by people using distinctive Beaker pottery. Active occupation of the site appears to have then lapsed for around two thousand years until the time of the Iron Age Celts. Around the time of Christ, Knowth was again used as a burial place, this time not for cremations but for burials. There were 35 burials and, interestingly, the majority of the graves belonged to women. Another grave contained the remains of two young men. They had been buried together with a set of gaming pieces. Like the people of the earlier Stone Age, whose bones are found in the tombs, these young men's story has been lost forever.

Following this period, Knowth never regained its function as a sacred place and was transformed into a place where people lived. From then on, through the Iron Age, Early Christian period and on into the Middle Ages, Knowth was used as a fortified dwelling place.

In about 300 AD, a Celtic chieftain had his workers dig two huge ditches around the mound, one at the base and one nearer the top. This project was a major undertaking – the lower ditch cuts 3m into the bedrock and must have been as costly in terms of resources and investment as the building of the original mound had been to the Neolithic farmers at the site some 3000 years earlier. The Neolithic people had lived in peaceful times. The ditches tell a story of troubled and violent times.

Over the centuries that followed, people continued to live on the mound. Somewhat more peaceful times may be evident in the fact that the deep ditches were allowed to silt up.

The following few centuries are known as the Early Christian period and these saw a substantial population living at the site. Houses with underground passages and chambers known as souterrains were built on and around the hillside. These souterrains were of various sizes and resembled the earlier Neolithic tombs but were used as storehouses. During times of attack there is evidence that they were also used as places of refuge. Archaeologists have found the remains of thirteen houses dating to the Early Christian era. Although small by today's standards, this represents a major settlement. The settlement attracted the attention of raiders, both native and foreign. The Vikings sailed their boats up the Boyne and ransacked the 'cave' of Knowth several times in the ninth and tenth centuries.

A branch of the southern Uí Néill became rulers of the Celtic kingdom of North Brega and made Knowth their capital in the ninth century AD. At this time in Ireland there were about 150 local kings, each one vying to be High King of Ireland at Tara. One of the kings based at Knowth, Congalach Mac Maelmithic, or Congalach Cnobha, succeeded in acquiring the high kingship in the mid-tenth century.

In the twelfth century, the lands around Knowth were granted to the new Cistercian abbey at Mellifont in County Louth. When the Normans came to Ireland, the mound of Knowth was converted into a motte. Archaeologists found the remains of a rectangular stone structure on the mound's summit which had been built using mortar — the first evidence of mortar in 5000 years of building, rebuilding and alterations. When the Tudor monarchs came to power in England, the abbey was dissolved and its lands were taken from the monks and handed over to supporters of the British Crown. Knowth continued to be used as a habitation site and there is evidence of sixteenth and seventeenth-century farmhouses. Knowth was granted official protection in 1882 and the Irish government eventually purchased the monument and surrounding lands. In 1962, before Professor Eogan began the excavation of the site, the mound was being used for grazing cattle.

Like most areas and monuments in Ireland, Knowth owes the origin of its name to legend and folklore. In Celtic times Knowth was known by the Irish form of its name, Sí Cnogba. There are many stories about Sí Cnogba in the old sagas. One of these relates a tale about Aonghus, the god of love and son of the Dagda, the most prominent of the older Celtic gods, and of Boann, the goddess of the river Boyne. Aonghus, who was very handsome, was the protector of lovers. Four birds, which represented his kisses, always hovered around his head. One day, when he was holding a feast in his palace at Sí an Bhrú (Newgrange), the girl he loved was abducted by his enemies. Aonghus sent his warriors off in pursuit but they failed to overtake the girl and her abductors. When the warriors stopped to rest at Knowth, the only food they could find to eat was nuts. These they ate while lamenting the missing girl. According to the legend, the word *cnogba* (the nut lamentation) derives from this incident.

Dowth

The name Dowth comes from *dubad*, the old Irish word for darkness. Its full name in Irish is Sí Dubhaidh, meaning the Fairy Mound of Darkness. According to legend it was built by King Bressal Bodibad, who put all the men of Ireland under a spell for one day so that they would build a mound for him that would reach up to the firmament. He persuaded his sister, who was a sorceress, to use her magic powers to halt the sun in the sky so that the day would not end. However, during that long day he offended his sister and darkness immediately fell upon the land. The darkness broke the spell the men were under and they left the site at once. From that day onward, the legend says, the site was known as Sí Dubhaidh.

Dowth is roughly the same size as its neighbours Newgrange and Knowth but has remained unexcavated in recent times. The monument is situated on a hill overlooking the river Boyne about a kilometre from Newgrange. The mound measures about 84m in diameter and is higher and more conical than Newgrange. Unlike Newgrange and Knowth,

PLAN OF DOWTH

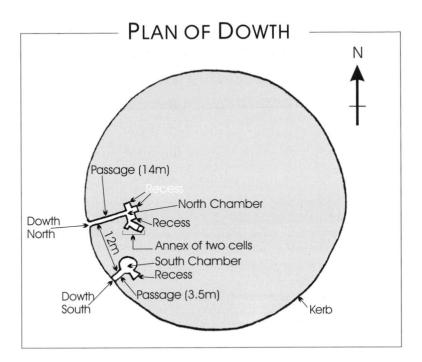

N

Passage (14m)

Recess

North Chamber

Dowth North

Recess

12m

Annex of two cells

South Chamber

Recess

Dowth South

Passage (3.5m)

Kerb

there is no evidence for standing stones around Dowth. When Sir William Wilde visited the mound in 1837 there was a building standing on top of it. He described it as:

> 'a modern structure, a tea-house erected by the late eccentric Lord Netterville; and, certainly, although his knowledge or love for antiquities may be questioned, there can be no doubt of his having chosen a spot from whence could be obtained one of the noblest prospects in Meath.'

Dowth was first excavated in 1847 and, like Knowth, was found to contain two separate passage tombs. These are small in comparison to those at the other main Boyne monuments and are both on the western side of the mound. The more northerly of these tombs is the most striking. It is cruciform in shape with an annex off the right-hand recess consisting of two cells. There is a single stone basin on the floor of the main chamber, but it is believed that this has been moved and was originally placed in the large recess to the right.

Unlike the high vault roofs in Newgrange and Knowth East, the chamber has a modest corbelled roof only 3m in height. The builders of Dowth North used four tall pillars to

The unexcavated mound of Dowth.

outline the walls of the central chamber, leaving four gaps between for the passage and recesses. Professors Michael Herity and George Eogan note that this design was later used by the builders of the passage tombs at Loughcrew in County Meath and at Carrowkeel and Carrowmore in County Sligo.

The smaller, southern tomb at Dowth has a short passage, only 3.5m long, leading into a circular chamber which also had a corbelled roof. This collapsed in ancient times and has now been replaced by a concrete roof. There is one recess leading off to the right of the chamber. In recent years, people have visited Dowth South to witness the sunlight entering the tomb at sunset on the winter solstice. Although there is no roof-box as at Newgrange, the effect is still very dramatic.

Debris of quartz stone was found outside the line of kerbstones surrounding the tomb, suggesting that originally Dowth may have had the same impressive white façade that we now see at Newgrange.

The art at Dowth is less sophisticated than that of its two more famous neighbours but includes the familiar lozenge, chevron and spiral designs. There are fewer carvings and the picking is usually lighter and more difficult to see. Dowth still has some outstanding examples of Megalithic art, notably the seven 'sun symbols' on K51 and the art on the last stone on the right-hand side of Dowth North's passage, which cleverly uses the edge of the stone to accentuate the rays of a wonderfully carved 'sunburst'.

During the initial excavation in 1847 some interesting articles were found, but the excavators did not catalogue their finds or prepare a scientific report. The finds included burnt and unburnt human bones and animal bones, glass and amber beads, rings, knives and portions of jet bracelets. Unfortunately, much damage was caused to the site by the unprofessional methods of the persons who carried out that excavation.

Dowth, like its neighbour Knowth, survived as a settlement for thousands of years. However, it appears to have been considered less important than Knowth and there are few references to it in the various annals. According to the Annals of Tighearnach, Abbot of Clonmacnoise, the settlement on or beside the mound was burned by King Conchúir Ó Maolsheachlainn in AD 1059. The Annals of the Four Masters state that it was burned and plundered again in AD 1170 by Dermot MacMurrough, King of Leinster.

Despite these attacks, the botched excavations of 1847 and the attempt some years later to use some of its stones for road paving, Dowth survived. The site is not open to the public at present but, as the Irish government has recently purchased it, that may soon change.

CHAPTER FOUR

The Art of Brú na Bóinne

The ornamentation of the stones inside and outside the monument is one of the most fascinating and evocative features of Newgrange. The significance of these patterns, whether religious, astronomical or otherwise, has so far defied all attempts at interpretation. But what is generally accepted is that, for the people who built the monuments 5000 years ago, the symbols had a deep significance. For the people who visit the monument today, the art is one of the great points of interest.

Most of the carving of the stones for the tomb would have been completed before the stones were positioned in their final resting places. However, some of the more spectacular stones, like the entrance stone and K52, were carved *after* they were put into place. The techniques employed by the artists differed according to the result they wanted to achieve. Only very rarely would the artist simply drag a stone point across the stone to make the design required.

Tapping a flint or quartz point with a heavy stone hammer (a maul) created the patterns on most of the carved stones. This was basic hammer-and-chisel work. The effect of this type of carving is a picked-out area of design. Sometimes the picking is coarse and the art seems inexpert, while in other instances the picking is very fine and the result is very skilful. The most difficult technique must have been that used to make the pattern in relief, that is, to make it seem as if the design is standing out from the stone on which it is carved. The wonderful ornamentation on the entrance stone and on K52 was made this way.

THE CARVINGS INSIDE NEWGRANGE

On entering the passage, as the eyes adjust to the darkness, one becomes aware that many of the stones which make up the walls of the passage are wonderfully carved. The first carving most visitors notice is on the right. It has two broad bands of picking right across its surface. Most people have the urge to run their hands over the stone's surface and one cannot help wondering about the significance of this design for the artist who carved it.

The next stone noticed is further up the passage on the left. It could almost be a mask-like representation of a human face. The hair of the mask is a zigzag pattern and the eyes are a double spiral, the nose is a lozenge and the gaping mouth is another spiral. This stone is just at the point where the passage bends towards the chamber and some people think it was deliberately placed there to frighten those who were entering the tomb. Some are so convinced that it represents a face that they refer to this stone as the Guardian Stone and

The 'Guardian Stone' in Newgrange.

believe that it proves that the tomb has a guardian spirit who watches over the remains of those housed there.

As one enters the chamber, the final carved stone that catches the eye is the last one on the right. This stone has several broad bands picked across it as well as deep, round hollows and lozenges at the top. Long ago, when children visited the tomb they were told by the caretaker that a giant had once lived inside Newgrange and that he was so big and fat that the bands were the tracks of his ribs as he squeezed in.

In the chamber itself, the most astonishing stone is the roof stone in the right-hand recess. It is covered with a profusion of energetic designs. They swirl, curl and twist across the entire surface of the stone and even beyond the visible surface.

Two other sets of carvings are immediately apparent: the spirals on the back wall of the left-hand recess and the lozenges and diamonds that are carved on the front edges of some of the corbels. Although there is relatively little ornamentation in the back recess, it does contain one of the most famous designs in Megalithic art. This consists of three carved spirals, a tri-spiral, intertwined on the lower portion of the stone (a symbol which has been reproduced again and again and is probably the symbol that is most closely associated with Newgrange). This famous motif is not as prominent as one would expect. The stone on which it is carved has broken at the base and tilts forward, so that if you are standing in the centre of the chamber it is hidden from view.

Long before the excavations began in 1962, there had been a story told that on certain days of the year (nobody could say

just when) sunlight fell on this tri-spiral design. Professor O'Kelly was familiar with the tale when he started his work. He thought that the tale confused Newgrange with the well-known alignment at Stonehenge. However, he recalled the story when the roof-box was rediscovered.

Two passage stones, the last on the right before the chamber. The stone on the left bears the imprint of the giant's ribs.

The Newgrange monument dominating the landscape of the valley of the river Boyne.

The entrance stone is a delicate, precise and beautiful example of Megalithic art.
The roof-box is visible behind it.

The chamber at Newgrange, with the tri-spiral design visible on the left.

The light of the winter solstice sun flooding the passage and chamber.

Dowth, as yet unexcavated.

Brú na Bóinne Visitor Centre, the starting-point for tours of the Boyne Valley monuments.

The north chamber at Dowth.

The central mound at Knowth surrounded by three of its eighteen satellite tombs.

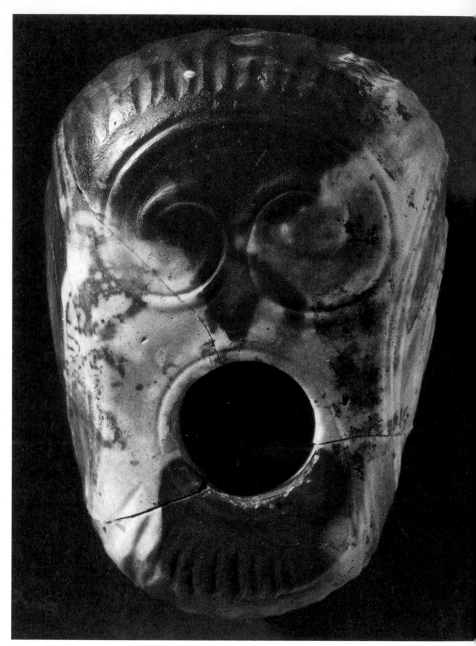

The haunting, exquisitely carved flint mace head unearthed during excavations at Knowth.

A Stone Age artist using a 'hammer-and-chisel' technique to carve designs on a stone. The stone will be put in place when he has finished his work. Behind him, the builders have begun their work on the tomb according to the guiding line of the wooden posts.

He found by experiment that the beam of light that penetrates the chamber at dawn on the winter solstice reaches the

The famous tri-spiral design from the chamber at Newgrange.

floor of the chamber just below the tri-spiral. No one in modern times could possibly have seen the light in the chamber before Professor O'Kelly, as the roof-box had been blocked up with large stones and covered over by the collapsed walls of the cairn. It seems incredible that the story, for so long considered an old wives' tale, was proved right.

THE ART OF KNOWTH AND DOWTH

It is interesting to compare the art of Newgrange with that of its neighbouring tombs at Knowth and Dowth. The director of the ongoing excavations at Knowth, Professor George Eogan, asserts that Knowth possesses Europe's greatest concentration of Megalithic art. Knowth has a greater number of expertly carved kerbstones than Newgrange and Dowth put together. The art is so prolific that Professor Eogan likens it to a great outdoor art gallery.

There is a different 'feel' to the art at each of the monuments. The art at Newgrange seems somehow formal and stylised, while the art at Dowth is fervent in execution yet unsophisticated by comparison. The carvings at Knowth have more flair, are bolder and more confident. Two particularly beautiful objects found in Knowth, a mace head and a stone basin, epitomise the level of skill attained by the artists there. The magnificent stone basin, elaborately carved, is considered to be one of the finest examples of its kind.

It is easy to imagine Stone Age people gathering at Knowth twice a year for the equinox celebrations. They went there after the crops were sown, before they were harvested. Of the three tombs, Knowth seems somehow most connected to the rhythms of the earth and the preoccupations of a farming community than the other monuments. It is a place to celebrate the more ordinary achievements of the Boyne culture, a place to gather in day-long celebration of the good earth and its fertility.

The 'Guardian Stone' from Knowth West.

The art reflects this with its strong lines and use of the stones' natural contours. The many stone settings on the ground in front of the two entrances suggest that many ceremonies took place. (Stone settings are the paved areas on the ground outside the entrances, some circular, some u-shaped.) Perhaps the leaders of the community brought the carved mace head from

Decorated stone from Dowth.

inside the eastern chamber to 'speak' to the people after the rising sun had illuminated it. As the day wore on, the secrets of the art on the kerbstones may have been revealed and interpreted.

At the end of the day, the sun entered the western tomb and the shadow of the large standing stone penetrated the long passage as the sun set. Perhaps this was a symbol that the earth would remain fertile and continue to sustain the community.

MEANINGS AND MYSTERIES

The precise meanings of the engravings at the monuments will never be known. Do the designs hold clues which, if decoded, could tell us more about this remarkable culture? Are the carvings sacred inscriptions with special, religious significance?

One thing is certain, no matter how we try to analyse or make sense of the art, we cannot see the world as our ancestors saw it 5000 years ago. If we were able to travel back to the Stone Age, we would not see different things from our Stone Age ancestors, but we would certainly see things differently.

In our time, we know that the earth travels around the sun because science has shown this to be true. We know that when the dark days of winter are with us that they will end and that spring will eventually come. We put magic, science, art and religion in separate boxes. In the Stone Age, all these things were probably 'in the same box'. The world was whole, all events related to each other, and time was an ever-repeating cycle. For us in the twentieth century, time and life are understood as a progression from A to B, a straight line. But the people who built these imposing monuments lived an existence governed by cycles, so time and life would have been understood in terms of a continual circle.

Some of the mysterious symbols from the interior of Dowth, recorded by Sir William Wilde.

Most visitors to Newgrange say that they feel the spiral designs represent the sun. If somehow we could prove that this is true – that the artists had indeed intended to

represent the sun with their spirals and concentric circles –
we would still need to know what the sun meant to the artist.
This is an indication of the kind of problems any would-be
interpreter faces.

Despite the obvious barriers to understanding the world
as our ancestors did, and given the enormous lapse of intervening time, there are countless speculators who claim to
have solved the meaning of Newgrange by deciphering its
artwork. We are constantly presented with a bewildering
array of theories and answers to unanswerable questions.

The facts are that a basic, early farming society, using rudi-
mentary technology, erected a number of enduring and
ever-fascinating monuments in the Boyne Valley some 5000
years ago. They did this using their own creativity and
strength, motivated by a deep spiritual conviction. They did
not, as some suggest, get help from aliens and did not levitate
the stones into position using magic. Such suggestions serve
only to detract from the immensity of their achievements in
the Boyne Valley.

We know from the alignments of various monuments that
the builders had a great interest in and knowledge of astron-
omy. The most widely accepted interpretation of the symbols
is the most obvious one — that the art represents a fascination
with the changing seasons and how the cycles related to their
own lives.

A second theory is that the carvings on the stones are actually maps. Sometimes the maps are said to be of the local area.
In this explanation, the spirals represent the mounds, the

A carving from Newgrange known as the Solar Boat. This refers to a popular theory, in vogue in the first half of this century, that the carving represents a boat, and that the circle above it on the left represents the sun.

curving lines mark rivers and the lozenges mark the ancient field systems. Other theorists suggest that the art represents maps of the other world or afterlife. Others again have read the stones as maps of the stars, sometimes to show us the planet or the star system that the builders came from! The art has also been interpreted as maps of the moon.

Another theory, highly regarded in academic circles, suggests that the symbols represent images seen by the holy men or women when they used hallucinogenic drugs to help them travel to the other world. Scientific research has proven that images seen and described by those under the influence of certain drugs are very like those designs carved at Newgrange and at the other monuments. Other suggestions include the notion that the carved stones may have been used as meditation devices or that they represent music or energy lines. All in all, most people find in Newgrange what they want to find.

A story has been told that links the entrance stone at Newgrange with Celtic legend. It shows that people have been musing on the meanings of its art for a long time. The story goes that Fionn Mac Cumhaill, the great leader of the Fianna, was on the Hill of Tara one day when he was angered by one of his enemies. He took up a stone to throw at his enemy and being the giant of a man he was, he took a very large stone. He flung it at his foe, but his strength was so great that the stone went flying by the fortunate target and travelled right down the Boyne Valley before it came to rest at the entrance to Newgrange. There it remains, bearing his fingerprints.

CHAPTER FIVE

The End of an Era
and a New Beginning

WHAT HAPPENED TO THE BOYNE SETTLERS?
With the passing of time, the society that built Newgrange went into decline. Nobody can say for certain what happened to the Boyne community. The 'classical' period of passage tombs in the Boyne Valley lasted perhaps some five or six hundred years. Then other cultures and traditions, like the Beaker culture, evolved in the Boyne Valley. There is no consensus as to how and why this occurred and the Beaker 'problem' has been, and remains, a source of contention among archaeologists.

Some archaeologists suggest that the arrival, around 2000 BC, of an Early Bronze Age community, known as the Beaker people, culminated in the expulsion of the Boyne people from their homes and their land. It is possible that the Beaker People decided to take the Boyne Valley for themselves and forcibly evicted the Neolithic settlers from the area. Alternatively, the Beaker People may have been a peaceful people who brought knowledge of new technologies and shared their knowledge with their new neighbours. In this way, the existing Neolithic Boyne culture would simply have been absorbed by, rather than replaced by the Bronze Age community.

A third theory suggests that Beaker people never actually came to the Boyne Valley but rather Beaker ideas and objects, which could have been circulated via trading connections. The basis of this line of thought is that the Beaker culture in Ireland simply does not conform to that of the rest of Europe. As Dr Peter Harbison outlines in *Pre-Christian Ireland*, the Beaker cultural phenomenon reaches from Hungary to Portugal and from Denmark to Sicily. All through this vast area there is a 'sameness' about the way Beaker artefacts are used. In continental Europe and Britain, Beaker pottery is mostly associated with burials. However, in Ireland the pottery is primarily associated with domestic use. If Beaker people had come to Ireland, why would they have used typical Beaker artefacts in completely different ways to those of contemporary Beaker cultures on the continent? This discrepancy supports the suggestion that their influence was by indirect means.

THE BEAKER PERIOD

The Beaker period coincides with the beginning of the Bronze Age (around 2000 BC). The term 'Beaker' refers to the finely made pottery vessels or beakers used by this culture. Beaker pottery has distinctive thin walls and elaborate decorations. The ornamentation of the pottery is achieved with a short-tooth comb and is characterised by zigzag geometric patterns. There are alternating patches of plain and decorated areas across the surface.

Although stone tools continued to be used at this time, they were gradually replaced by the rise of metalworking. Beaker groups knew how to find and extract metal ore from the ground. These prospectors were also smiths, and by blending tin with copper they produced the harder alloy called bronze. They were, of course, also farmers and several novelties were introduced into Ireland at this time, including, for the first time, horses.

By the time the Beaker people were living beside Newgrange it had already fallen into disuse as a tomb. Its entrance was completely blocked by the collapsing mound. That is not to say that Newgrange played no part in the daily life of the new culture. The monument continued to be a focal point for ritual gatherings. Within 10m of the ancient passage tomb a massive circular enclosure was constructed, now called a woodhenge or pit circle. Excavations have shown it to have been a large double circle of wooden posts (about 100m in diameter), inside which animals were cremated and buried in pits.

MEGALITHIC HENGES

A henge is a circular monument composed of uprights made of wood or stone, therefore we refer to a woodhenge or a stone-henge. Circle patterns of all sorts are very common at prehistoric sites and have been the object of much speculation as to their function and meaning. For our prehistoric ancestors, henges may have held a religious significance. This theory is supported by examples like Stonehenge in England, which is built according to the trajectory of the rising sun on the summer solstice.

It seems that the wood-henge served as a religious centre, as important in its day as the huge passage tomb had been about a thousand years earlier.

The henges of the Boyne (there was also an enormous earthen structure close to Dowth), were roughly contemporary with similar Beaker sites in the south of England. One such wooden ritual site at Salisbury Plain in Wiltshire was replaced, at great expense to its community, with an amazing structure in stone – Stonehenge. It is the Bronze Age's foremost statement of power, confidence and ingenuity, just as Newgrange was for the Neolithic period.

THE STONE CIRCLE

A circle of twelve standing stones surrounds the great mound at Newgrange. Originally, there may have been more, but if so they were removed long ago. Following the excavation of the wood-henge, it became apparent that the stone circle had been erected some time after 2000 BC. One of the stones actually sits on top of the pits of the wood-henge, making it obvious that it was placed there later. The purpose of the stone circle is not clear but research indicates that it could have had an astronomical function. In any case, it was the final stage of building at Newgrange.

With the coming of the Celts, Newgrange was transformed into a house for their deities. Brú na Bóinne is featured in many of the great Celtic myths. As a dwelling place of the deities, it was revered by visitors from Roman Britain even as late as AD 400. Their votive offerings of coins and jewellery were recovered from the top of the mound during excavations.

An aerial view of Newgrange showing the remains of the stone circle.

CHAPTER SIX

Rediscovery and Reconstruction

For many centuries Newgrange lay abandoned in obscurity and disrepair. To the casual onlooker it seemed to be merely a large, insignificant mound of earth overgrown with grass. The ownership of the land on which Newgrange stood passed through various hands after the confiscations in the reign of Henry VIII. By 1699, it was in the possession of Charles Campbell. That year, something happened that was to lead to the opening of a new chapter in the story of Newgrange.

Campbell was looking for ready stones for building purposes and knew there were many loose stones on the hill at Newgrange. He sent his workers to begin collecting stones, unaware that a chamber holding the remains of an ancient people lay within the mound. The workers soon uncovered a large boulder with unusual designs carved on it. No doubt Campbell was quickly sent for and was present when his men eventually uncovered the entrance to the tomb. Lighting a torch, he made his way down the passage until he reached the chamber – the first person to do so for many centuries.

Word of the discovery soon spread. The first written description of the rediscovered tomb came the same year from a Welshman, Edward Lhuyd. Lhuyd was a noted antiquarian and keeper of the Ashmolean Museum in Oxford. He was en route to the Giant's Causeway in County Antrim when he heard about the rediscovery of Newgrange. He went to view it, but was not impressed by the tomb:

> 'I also met with one monument in this kingdom; it stands at a place called Newgrange near Drogheda, and is a mount or barrow of very considerable height encompassed with vast stones pitched on end around the bottom of it... The entry into this cave is at bottom and before it we found a great flat stone like a large tomb-stone, placed edgeways, having on the outside barbarous carvings like snakes encircled but without heads.'

When Sir Thomas Molyneux, Professor of Physics in Trinity College, Dublin, visited the site shortly after Lhuyd's visit, he was equally dismissive of the great stone. He described it as a 'barbarous kind of carving, showing not the least footsteps of writing'.

The noted nineteenth-century antiquarian George Petrie was incensed by the failure of antiquarians in preceding centuries to recognise the true importance of Newgrange. He regarded them as being 'unwilling, apparently, to allow the ancient Irish the honour of erecting a work of such vast labour and grandeur, ascribing it to the piratical Danes who infested the island in the 8th and 10th centuries'.

When Sir William Wilde, the renowned oculist, noted anti-quarian and father of Oscar Wilde, visited Newgrange in 1837 he was immediately fascinated by the monument, despite its neglected appearance. He found the entrance 'greatly obscured by brambles and a heap of loose stones which had ravelled out from the adjoining mound'.

Wilde's sketch of the entrance to Newgrange as it looked in the nineteenth century.

After referring to Lhuyd's dismissive account of the great entrance stone, he described its true qualities as he saw them.

> 'This stone, so beautifully carved in spirals and volutes...is slightly convex from above downwards; it measures ten feet in length and is about eighteen inches thick. What its original use was —where its original position in this mound — whether its carvings exhibit the same handiwork and design as those sculptured stones in the interior, and whether this beautiful slab did not belong to some building of anterior date - are questions not now soluble.'

Newgrange and its surrounding lands have had many landowners since the time of Charles Campbell, some of them interested in antiquities and others less so. Farming over the centuries has destroyed many of the earthen enclosures and smaller mounds. When the Irish State purchased the land in 1961 it was the property of the Delaney family.

The noted Irish naturalist and antiquarian R. Lloyd Praeger visited Newgrange in the 1930s and described how cattle roaming about and over the mound had affected its condition. Praeger found that the kerb of slabs was buried to its upper edge by stones which had slid down from above. He took part in excavation work, which involved sinking a

Newgrange as it stands today, following restoration work
led by Professor Michael J. O'Kelly.

trench 2m deep through loose stones to reach the base of the kerb. This showed that all the sloping ground between the kerb and the surrounding field was made of material that belonged to the mound. We can imagine the formidable task that faced the archaeologists when work began on the excavation and restoration of Newgrange in 1962.

The excavation and restoration work was conducted by Professor M. J. O'Kelly of University College, Cork. For the restoration, special care was taken to ascertain the original shape of the mound in order to ensure that the result would be as authentic as possible. The original quartz stones of the façade, which had collapsed forward, were picked up and replaced as the retaining wall or *revêtment*. The oval granite stones were also reset among the gleaming white quartz.

CONTROVERSY

Under the supervision of Professor O'Kelly, the restoration of Newgrange was completed in 1975. Its reconstruction was a remarkable achievement. The mound now stands restored to all its former glory. But, like many such achievements, the restoration has not been without some measure of controversy.

Critics have been divided on the validity of the reconstructed façade with its spectacular, shining quartz. Yet, in a descriptive passage from Silva Gadelica, a medieval Irish manuscript, Newgrange is recorded as being 'brilliant to approach'. There is no question but that the mound was originally faced with quartz and granite. The reasons why the ancient builders went to so much trouble to face their monument in this way is, of course, unclear. It could be that the stones were intended to make the monument visible from a great distance. It could just as well have been to reflect the glory of the sun deity, to concentrate energy, to signify death, or rebirth, or even as mere decoration. All, any, or a combination of these reasons could certainly be possible.

Some criticism has also been directed at the way the entrance area was rebuilt, chiefly because it does not conform to the original shape as the area behind the entrance stone is now scooped away. It would not have been practical to rebuild the area according to its original layout, as sufficient space would not then be available to allow adequate access for visitors to the tomb. This made it necessary to modify the entrance area by the addition of modern masonry walls.

In the face of all controversy, Professor O'Kelly stoutly defended his interpretation and methods. Professor O'Kelly was, perhaps above all, a practical archaeologist. In order to understand and experience the lives and activities of the Stone Age people he was studying, he cooked meat in an ancient cooking pit, he experimented by carving stones with flint points and he had his students move large slabs with authentic materials to see how it could have been done in the Stone Age. In order to prove the height and angle of the restored quartz *revêtment*, he rebuilt a section of wall and then knocked it down. The profile of the modern slippage was identical to the excavated ancient material.

We can understand now how it happened that neither Sir William Wilde nor any other antiquarians at that time were aware of the function of the roof-box. Wilde described how the edge of another 'most exquisitely carved stone' was found projecting from the mound a short distance above and within the line of the entrance. This 'lintel', as he called it, was approximately 1.5m long and he considered that its sculptured carvings, both in design and execution, far exceeded any of the examples found within the tomb itself. Wilde thought it likely that it heralded the entrance to another chamber 'which further examination may yet disclose'. This was, in fact, the roof-box, which would later prove to be the most exciting discovery during the mound's excavation.

In 1874 an antiquarian named Richard Burchett, who was investigating the site, reported that he had been unable to solve the mystery of the 'false lintel', despite having uncovered its whole surface. He said that he found 'two men with crowbars incapable of moving it without greater risk to its safety than I was willing to incur'. Luckily, the roof-box survived intact, which allowed Professor O'Kelly to unravel its purpose and invite us to appreciate the genius of our Stone Age ancestors.

There had long been a belief that on certain occasions sunlight penetrated into the passage at Newgrange. As the monument faces southeast, the possibility of its connection with the midsummer sunrise was ruled out. Professor

O'Kelly decided to test his theory that the structure of the tomb was in fact connected with the winter solstice, the shortest day of the year. On 21 December 1967, he was the first person for thousands of years to see the early rays of the solstice sun making their way into the passage of the tomb.

Professor O'Kelly was extremely lucky to witness this spectacle of light first time round. The occurrence of the phenomenon is, of course, dependent on weather conditions. In the event of cloud, the sun is not able to penetrate the tomb through the roof-box. A further potential problem is that the angle of sunlight is now different from what it would have been when Newgrange was built, due to the movement of the earth in relation to the sun over the intervening thousands of years.

Winter solstice at Newgrange.

In spite of all these potential problems, Professor O'Kelly's viewing of the spectacle was a success and the mystery of the roof-box was finally solved. He described how, on the morning of the solstice, the sun slowly began to rise and the first ray of sunlight came through the roof-box. The light shone across the floor of the chamber until it came to rest on the stone basin in the back recess. As the light grew stronger, the tomb was lit up. It was a unique and gratifying experience. (The full text of Professor O'Kelly's description is available in his seminal work, *Newgrange: Archaeology, Art and Legend*.)

DATING THE MONUMENT

Although the great pyramids of Egypt were once believed to predate Newgrange, it is now accepted that the reverse is in fact true. The date ascribed to Newgrange is c.3200 BC, but how do we know this? The method used by archaeologists involved radiocarbon dating of material found in the monument.

Archaeologists were able to test the material that the Stone Age builders had packed into gaps between the roofslabs. This material consisted of burnt clay and sea sand and had a putty-like consistency. Because the material contained carbon, scientists were able to determine its age by applying a technique known as radiocarbon dating. Radiocarbon or C-14 dating was discovered by Willard Libby, an American chemist, in 1949. The technique revolutionised archaeology and has become the standard method of dating organic remains and artefacts.

All organic material contains carbon. Just as there are light and heavy forms of oxygen molecules, there are also two forms of carbon molecule. Most carbon has twelve atoms and is known as C-12. Carbon also has a heavy, radioactive isotope known as Carbon 14 (C-14). C-14 is present as a gas in the atmosphere and is absorbed by all living organisms at a known rate. When an organism dies or, for example, when a piece of pottery containing carbon is fired at great temperatures, it can no longer absorb this C-14. When this occurs, the radioactive carbon absorbed begins to decay and the rate of the decay can be measured. By measuring the amount of C-14 in a bone, plant or pot, experts can determine the age of the object.

Radiocarbon dating shows the age of material in what are known as radiocarbon years. Radiocarbon years are more recent than our calendar years so a scientific system is used to convert them into calendar years. The radiocarbon date given for Newgrange is 2500 bc, this translates to c.3200 BC when converted to our present calendar.

TIMELINE

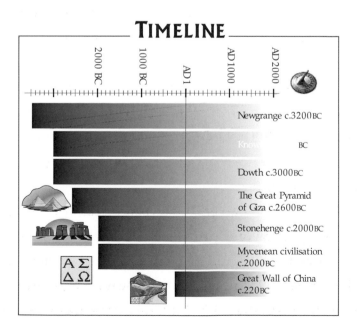

2000 BC   1000 BC   AD 1   AD 1000   AD 2000

Newgrange c.3200 BC

Kno... BC

Dowth c.3000 BC

The Great Pyramid of Giza c.2600 BC

Stonehenge c.2000 BC

Mycenean civilisation c.2000 BC

Great Wall of China c.220 BC

FINDS FROM NEWGRANGE

When Edward Lhuyd visited the monument shortly after its rediscovery, what had been found within the chamber when it was first opened had already become hearsay. He mentions that human bones as well as pieces of antler were found. He also mentions the discovery of two gold Roman coins. Thomas Molyneux also mentioned the coins following his visit to Newgrange some years later, but these have since disappeared without trace. Molyneux added the description of two skeletons on the floor of the tomb 'entire not buried'.

When Sir William Wilde visited Newgrange around 1837, he reported that 'under foot there were nothing but loose stones of every size in confusion, and amongst them a great many bones of beasts and some pieces of deer's horns'. In 1842 it was reported that a local labourer had found five gold ornaments buried near the entrance to Newgrange. Those ornaments are now on permanent display in the British Museum. Further searches uncovered more Roman coins, but these subsequently disappeared.

In 1863, during the removal of a pile of debris near the entrance, a gold band was found. This was decorated with a floral pattern on the front and engraved lines on the back. Four years later, another Roman coin was discovered.

When the tomb was excavated in the 1960s more Roman coins were found, as well as two disc brooches and finger rings of gold, silver and bronze. Also found were bone dice, a bronze bracelet and pin, and a strap loop of bronze engraved with a design in the La Tène style. (Celtic art of the Late Iron Age is commonly called La Tène after a well-known site in Switzerland.)

Where did the Roman coins come from? There were certainly trading links and other contacts between Ireland, Roman Britain and the continent in the third and fourth centuries AD which would explain the presence of the coins. They could be booty carried by Irish warriors returning from raiding expeditions, or gifts from foreign visitors on their way to Tara. Whatever their origin, they were probably deposited as offerings to the Celtic gods associated with the mound.

Despite the damage caused and the many unrecorded artefacts taken away over the centuries by amateur antiquarians and treasure seekers, further finds were made when the passage and chamber were excavated in the 1960s. Among these were human bones, burnt and unburnt, thought to have been originally located in the stone basins in the recesses. There were also many other finds outside the tomb. These included fragments of pottery, arrowheads and various implements made of flint. All of these artefacts have contributed to our understanding of the thriving and diverse communities of the area.

CHAPTER SEVEN

Other Boyne Valley Sites

While Newgrange, Knowth and Dowth are the three main prehistoric sites in the Boyne Valley, there are many other such sites in the area. In addition to the satellite tombs which surround Newgrange and Knowth, there are more than twenty other sites, such as standing stones, enclosures, ring forts and medieval field systems and weirs.

It was not only in ancient times that the Boyne Valley attracted new settlers and new ideas. Since the time of the early farmers, the valley has witnessed dynamic, if not always peaceful changes of populations and cultures. The remnants of these many stories are all around us. Some of the many sites of historical interest in the area of the Boyne Valley include the Hill of Tara, Old Mellifont Abbey, Bective Abbey and Monasterboice.

The Hill of Tara

Tara, lying 10km northeast of Trim in County Meath, is famous as the place where many of the high kings of Ireland reigned. The most famous of these was Cormac Mac Airt who brought Tara to the pinnacle of its glory in the third century AD. A ring fort within the huge hill fort known as the Royal

Enclosure on the Hill of Tara bears his name: Cormac's House. Beside Cormac's House there is a mound known as The Forradh, or Royal Seat, which is actually a prehistoric tomb. On top of The Forradh is the Lia Fáil – the Stone of Destiny. The Lia Fáil is an ancient fertility symbol. Legend has it that on the inauguration of a worthy high king the stone would roar its approval, thus sealing the fate of the fortunate candidate. Another monument on the Hill of Tara is called Gráinne's Enclosure, which reminds us that it was at Tara that the great Celtic saga of Diarmaid and Gráinne began. Tara is also where St Patrick began his missionary work.

At the time of the high kings, Tara was largely a ceremonial and religious centre. The kings of Tara never lived there. They had a number of taboos placed on them at their inauguration, reflecting the ritual and sacred nature of the kingship. One of these obligations was that the kings were never to let the sun rise on them in Tara.

THE HIGH KINGS OF IRELAND

For centuries Ireland was composed of many small 'kingdoms' ruled over by a chieftain or king. There was a loose hierarchy with the High King or Árd Rí at its head. The residence of the High King was at the royal palace of Tara. The position of High King was open to challenge. The high kingship alternated between the northern Uí Néill and the southern Uí Néill for centuries, until they were challenged, in the tenth century, by the most famous High King of all, Brian Boru, ruler of North Munster. Brian reigned as High King until his death, while leading the Irish against the invading Vikings, at the Battle of Clontarf in 1014.

The mounds, banks and great enclosures are no longer as imposing as they would have been and it does take imagination to picture the ancient capital of Celtic Ireland. Tara was

The Hill of Tara, the seat of the High Kings of Ireland.

abandoned by the High King Murchad Ó Maeilsheachlainn in AD 1022 and it quickly fell into the realms of pagan antiquity as Christianity took a firm hold in Ireland.

Mellifont Abbey

Old Mellifont Abbey is located in the valley of the river Mattock, a tributary of the river Boyne. It was the first Cistercian monastery to be established in Ireland (AD 1142). Its founder was a man of great charisma and dedication: St Malachy, the Archbishop of Armagh. Malachy had visited the monastery of Clairvaux in France and was greatly influenced by the Cistercian monks he met there, particularly St Bernard. After his experiences in Clairvaux, Malachy wanted to create a centre for Cistercian spiritual life in Ireland.

The success of Mellifont Abbey resulted in the establishing of several other Cistercian abbeys to accommodate the constant stream of willing novices. By the mid-twelfth century,

Mellifont had eleven daughter houses, an incredible achievement for a single monastic centre. When Mellifont was consecrated in 1157 it was a day of great pomp and celebration, with kings and bishops in attendance.

With the dissolution of the abbeys, Mellifont Abbey was suppressed by King Henry VIII in 1539 and the buildings and lands were taken from the monks. The lands and buildings came into the possession of the Moore family who converted the abbey buildings into a large mansion. It was at this house that Hugh O'Neill surrendered to the English after the defeat of his army at the Battle of Kinsale in 1603.

Today, the ruins of the abbey are a popular attraction in the Boyne Valley. The remains of the church, refectory, infirmary, chapter house and lavabo have survived. The lavabo originally contained a fountain at which the monks performed their ablutions before dining.

The remains of the lavabo at Old Mellifont Abbey.

Bective Abbey

The Cistercian complex of Bective Abbey, situated about 6km from the Norman stronghold of Trim, was the first daughter house of Old Mellifont Abbey. Though small in comparison, it was wealthy and influential. It was founded by Murchad Ó Maeilsheachlainn, King of Meath, in AD 1147. In 1536 it was dissolved by King Henry VIII, one of the first abbeys to fall foul of his suppression of the monasteries in Ireland.

Monasterboice

Monasterboice is the site of an Early Christian monastic settlement founded by St Buite Mac Bronaigh in AD 520. The historic ruins include a round tower and three high crosses famed for their exquisite artistry. The abbey was abandoned some time after 1122.

The round tower is still in relatively good condition. It was built as a bell tower but also served as a haven for the monks, protecting them and their sacred vessels and manuscripts from marauding bands of thieves and invaders, native and foreign. However, the tower was burnt in 1097 and its manuscripts and treasures were lost to the flames. The records for

SAINT PATRICK AND THE BOYNE VALLEY

After his return to Ireland, probably in AD 432, with the aim of converting the people to Christianity, St Patrick went to the Hill of Slane on the banks of the river Boyne. There, in sight of the High King's palace at Tara, he lit a great fire on the eve of Easter to celebrate the death and resurrection of Christ. This defiant act incurred the anger of the King, Laoghaire, and his druids. Patrick and his companions were captured and taken to Tara. There, he impressed the High King so favourably, he was granted permission to preach the new faith anywhere he wished in Ireland.

that period do not indicate the cause of the fire.

Two of the high crosses on the abbey grounds are considered the finest examples in Ireland: St Muireadach's Cross and the West or Tall Cross. Both are scriptural crosses, that is, they depict scenes from the Holy Scriptures.

St Muireadach's Cross stands 5.5m high and is finely carved over its entire surface. There is an inscription on the base of the cross which asks passers-by to offer up a prayer for Muireadach, 'by whom was made this cross'. The east-facing side of the cross shows the story of Adam and Eve, the murder of Abel by his brother, Cain, the epic battle between

Muireadach's Cross, Monasterboice, the most famous high cross in Ireland.

David and Goliath and the Last Judgement of the souls of the dead. The west-facing side depicts the Arrest of Christ, the 'Doubting Thomas' episode, Christ with Peter and Paul and the Crucifixion. The sculpture is exquisitely crafted in every detail and the cross is deservedly renowned as one of Ireland's finest.

Standing a few metres away from St Muireadach's Cross is the West or Tall Cross. The reason for its name is obvious – it stands 7m high, making it the tallest high cross in Ireland.

Passage tombs

Tombs comparable to those of the Brú na Bóinne complex are also found beyond the Boyne Valley. One example is the fascinating Megalithic cemetery at Loughcrew in northwest Meath, about 40km from Newgrange. This is another complicated site, consisting of approximately 30 passage tombs of various sizes dating to around 3000 BC. In Irish, Loughcrew is known as Sliabh na Caillighe, the Hill of the Witch. There are also passage tombs at Carrowmore and Carrowkeel in County Sligo, as well as smaller groups in other parts of Ireland.

Passage tombs in the Boyne tradition are also found outside of Ireland. They are associated with coastal, north and western Europe. There are closely related monuments in southern Sweden, Denmark, The Netherlands, Brittany, Spain and Portugal. The nearest relatives to the Boyne tombs are those found in Orkney, off the coast of Scotland, and Anglesey in Wales.

CHAPTER EIGHT

Newgrange in Celtic Lore

Despite the decline in the Boyne passage tomb culture and the deterioration of the mound itself, an atmosphere of mystery continued to envelop the great mound. Legends and stories grew around it as the tomb passed into folk memory, its mystery and power rekindled by colourful tales and dire warnings. The earliest of these concern the magical tribe of people known as the Tuatha Dé Danann.

The Tuatha Dé Danann

Tuatha Dé Danann means 'the people of the goddess Danu'. Unfortunately, beyond her name, little is known about the goddess Danu in Irish mythology. In some sources she is referred to as the mother of the three mythical brothers, Brian, Iucharba and Iuchar.

The Tuatha Dé Danann are mentioned in the Book of Invasions where they are described entering Ireland from overseas. Some legends state that they arrived by way of Norway and northern Scotland, led by their druids in a magic mist. They are said to have used their skills in magic to conquer the Fir Bolg, the people who were in Ireland before them. According to the Book of Invasions, the Tuatha Dé Danann were in turn conquered by a Celtic people called the Milesians who are supposed to have arrived in Ireland around 2000 BC.

Legend relates that the Tuatha Dé Danann chose to live underground in prehistoric tombs, such as Newgrange. It appears that imagined glimpses of the Tuatha Dé Danann, together with tales of their supposed magical powers, gave rise to the later tales of enchanted folk or fairies dwelling in the mound at Newgrange.

Diarmaid And Gráinne

One of the most romantic and exciting of the old Celtic tales is that known in Irish as *Toraíocht Dhiarmada agus Ghráinne* (The Hunt for Diarmaid and Gráinne). Aonghus and his palace at Newgrange play an important part in this tale of love, deception and vengeance.

Gráinne was the daughter of Cormac Mac Airt, the High King of Ireland. She was promised in marriage to Fionn Mac Cumhaill, the ageing leader of the Fianna – a band of warriors whose main role was to guard Ireland against invasion. To commemorate the occasion of the betrothal of Gráinne and Fionn, a great feast was held in the banqueting hall of the High King's palace at Tara in County Meath. During the feast, Gráinne saw and fell in love with a handsome young warrior, Diarmaid Ó Duibhne, who was one of Fionn's closest friends. Diarmaid was reluctant to become involved with Gráinne but she placed him under a magic spell and forced him to elope with her.

Seething with anger at their treachery, Fionn set out with his warriors in pursuit of the couple. However, the god Aonghus was Diarmaid's foster-father and when he heard what had happened, he protected Diarmaid from Fionn's attempts to kill him. Finally, Aonghus succeeded in making peace between Fionn and Diarmaid. The handsome young Diarmaid was by then deeply in love with Gráinne and made her his wife. But some years later, Diarmaid was hunting a wild boar and was seriously wounded by the animal. His only hope of recovery was for Fionn to use his magic healing skills to cure him. Still harbouring feelings of bitterness, Fionn refused to help and Diarmaid died. Filled with sorrow, Aonghus took the corpse of his beloved foster-son to Newgrange for burial.

THE FIANNA

According to tradition, in ancient Celtic Ireland the Fianna were the warriors who defended the High King and kept the peace. They were great hunters as well as warriors and were famed for their bravery, speed, knowledge and resourcefulness. Their base was at the Hill of Allen in County Kildare, but from May to November they travelled the country, usually sleeping under the stars. They were at their most formidable under the leadership of Fionn Mac Cumhaill, and it is from this time that the greatest of the great tales are told.

Cúchulainn

Also associated with Newgrange in Celtic mythology is Cúchulainn, one of the greatest of all the ancient heroes, whose brave feats are a colourful feature of *The Táin*, the most famous of the Irish sagas. According to legend, Cúchulainn was conceived in Newgrange and many of his adventures occurred in or near the Boyne Valley.

The Táin recounts how Cúchulainn single-handedly defended Ulster against the army of the redoubtable Queen Maeve of Connacht. The scheming queen had placed the Red Branch Knights of Ulster, the defenders of that kingdom, in an enchanted sleep in her efforts to capture the coveted Táin Bó Cuailgne, the White Bull of Cooley.

This famous tale, which has come down through many centuries of oral tradition, was probably first committed to writing around AD 800.

Cormac Mac Airt

Another famous figure in Celtic lore associated with Newgrange is Cormac Mac Airt, the reputed High King or Árd Rí of Ireland. He is said to have reigned from AD 227 to 266 and some sources consider that many of the traditional tales about him could in fact be authentic. According to the Book of Leinster, 'there was not in his time, nor before him, any more celebrated in honour and in dignity and in wisdom except Solomon, the son of David'.

Cormac's palace was at Tara, then the centre of royal power in Celtic Ireland. The Hill of Tara stands in the Boyne Valley, about 20km southwest of Newgrange. The renowned banqueting hall of the palace was said to measure 260m by 20m and to stand 16m high.

Aimergin Mac Amlaid, a scholar-bard of the seventh century, gives a poetic account of Cormac's royal household: the hall contained 150 beds, and 150 warriors stood in the king's presence when he sat down at a banquet. There were 150 cup-bearers, 150 jewelled cups of silver and gold and over 1000 people in the entire household. In the Book of Leinster, it is recorded that Cormac maintained 3000 persons in pay each day. It also states that many strangers from overseas came to see him, including Gauls, Romans and Franks, and that the High King presented them with gold and silver, horses and chariots in accordance with the ancient laws of hospitality. A seventeenth-century scholar and historian called O'Flaherty has recorded that 'Cormac exceeded all his predecessors in magnificence, generosity, wisdom and learning, as well as in military achievements'.

THE STORY OF A HIGH KING'S DEATH

The untimely death of Cormac Mac Airt is supposed to have occurred after Cormac turned against his druids and their pagan teachings and chose to follow the Christian doctrine. In revenge, one of the druids, Malgeen, invoked the help of the *Siabhradh* to bring about his death. The Siabhradh were evil spirits who were servants of the prehistoric demigods, the Tuatha Dé Danann. According to the Annals of the Four Masters, Cormac died in AD 266 by choking to death on a salmon bone – the mischievous work of the Siabhradh?

This remarkable king is said to have died about AD 267, more than a century and a half before St Patrick brought Christianity to Ireland. Although he lived in pagan times, Cormac Mac Airt, according to legend, had some inkling of the Christian faith some years before his death. An ancient tract called Relig na Ríogh, which is preserved in the Book of the Dun Cow, records that 'Cormac had the faith of the one true God...and said he would not adore stones or trees but would adore Him who made them'.

It is more likely, however, that this episode in his life story was an invention of later Christian authors in order to strengthen support for their relatively new religion. Because of the traditional fame and reputation of Cormac, his supposed association with the new faith would have enhanced its popular prestige.

Legend also states that, again inspired by Christianity, Cormac made a dying request that he should not be buried with pagan kings in the royal cemetery at Sí an Bhrú (Newgrange). Instead, he wished to be buried at Ros na Rí, southwest of Newgrange, facing where the holy light would dawn. However, the druids are said to have disregarded Cormac's dying wish and ordered that the king should be buried with his predecessors in the royal cemetery at Newgrange.

The funeral procession bearing his body set out from Tara towards the great mound. However, when they tried to cross the river Boyne, the river rose and prevented their crossing. Three attempts were made to cross the river. On the third attempt a great wave swelled up and swept the king's body away down the river. The waters cast his body up at Ros na Rí and there he was buried in accordance with his dying wish.

While it is fascinating to imagine the funerals of the high kings taking place at Newgrange, it is most unlikely that such events ever occurred at the tomb. Newgrange was nearly 3500 years old by the time Tara was at the height of its glory. By then the tomb would probably have been quite deteriorated. Again, the story of Cormac's burial could have been an invention to strengthen popular support for Christianity.

Superstitions

With the arrival and spread of Christianity in Ireland, belief in the old pagan deities gradually faded away. Nevertheless, Newgrange and other similar mounds were still regarded with suspicion and fear. One of the most enduring superstitions was that the tombs were the dwelling-places of the *slua sí* or fairy host.

The *slua sí* intruded on human life in many ways according to ancient beliefs. People believed that the *Sí* had the power to spirit a child from its cradle, leaving a fairy changeling in its place. The persistence of that superstition even up to recent times is exemplified in 'The Stolen Child', a poem by W.B. Yeats which describes how a fairy entices a human child away to the other world.

It was also believed that if a human came upon a band of the Little People, as the fairy host were also called, he or she would be placed under a spell and taken away to remain with them in their *lios* or underground home. We can imagine people's fear of such a fate when they passed by great mounds like Newgrange, especially in twilight or moonlight. Their fears are described by the poet William Allingham:

> *Up the airy mountain,*
> *Down the rushy glen,*
> *We daren't go a-hunting*
> *For fear of little men.*
> *They stole little Bridget*

for seven years long;
When she came down again
Her friends were all gone.

They took her lightly back,
Between the night and morrow,
They thought that she was fast asleep,
But she was dead with sorrow.

They have kept her ever since
Deep within the lake,
On a bed of flag-leaves,
Waiting till she wake.

The superstitious fear of the Little People and their mischievous ways is the subject of many poems and songs. 'Port na bPúcaí' (The Fairies' Lament) was noted down many years ago by Tomás Ó Dála of Inishvickilaun, one of the Blasket Islands off the south coast of County Kerry:

I will go then into the lios,
It is not a pleasant thing for me to do
but there I must go,
And leave everything in the world.

(Trans. Liam Mac Uistin)

It is easy to understand how the mounds assumed an imposing and forbidding aura. The eerie silence that pervades the tombs, the folklore tales about the underworld gods occupying the chambers and the deep-rooted dread of the Little People would all have served to ward people away from the tombs. It is easy to imagine local people hurrying down the lonely roads, past the massive humps of the tombs, whistling as they went to calm their fears. Our Neolithic ancestors may have been perfectly at ease with living in close proximity to the dead, but modern man is not so comfortable when the spirits of the departed threaten to stir from their sleep and wander forth in the deepening twilight.

Newgrange and the stone circle by the light of a harvest moon.

CHAPTER NINE

Newgrange Today

THE VISITOR CENTRE

Since the completion of its restoration in the mid-1970s, Newgrange has become a major tourist attraction. It has also become a focal point for our national identity. The famous tri-spiral has become a recognised symbol of Ireland both at home and abroad. Over the years, as the site became busier and busier, archaeologists, conservationists and the government became increasingly concerned about the effect the huge number of visitors was having on the fabric of the

Brú na Bóinne Visitor Centre at Donore, across the river from Newgrange.

monument. In 1987, Brú na Bóinne was declared an archaeological park by the government which means that all farming and building within the area is restricted. In 1993, UNESCO formally granted Newgrange and the other Boyne monuments the status of World Heritage Site.

It is understandable that this ancient and unique monument would be at risk if access to it were uncontrolled. Apart from the need to protect it from damage, it is common sense that access should be regulated so that its many visitors can view the tomb in reasonable comfort. The problem has been eased by the fine Brú na Bóinne Visitor Centre near Donore, across the river from Newgrange.

A display in the Visitor Centre showing various Neolithic implements.

The Department of Arts, Heritage, Gaeltacht and the Islands opened the Visitor Centre in 1997. It is now managed by the Office of Public Works. Each year it welcomes approximately 250,000 visitors, though not all of these actually visit the monument itself. The Visitor Centre provides an informative and stimulating interpretation of the archaeological sites in the Boyne Valley. It houses a comprehensive exhibition depicting the way of life of the Stone Age people who built Newgrange. There are reconstructed examples of their houses, clothing, boats, weapons, household implements and grave finds. In addition, a fascinating film shows in detail the solar alignments at Newgrange and Knowth. The highlight of the exhibition is a full-scale replica of the passage and chamber of Newgrange.

The Visitor Centre serves to whet our appetites for what awaits us at the mound itself. From the Centre, we cross the Boyne by pedestrian bridge and are taken by shuttle bus along country lanes to the great monument that dominates the valley. Then, we are brought inside the tomb, in small groups, to view its wonders at close range.

IMAGINING THE SUN

As we enter the passage and make our way into the chamber, we are filled with awe at the skills of those builders and artists working with primitive implements 5000 years ago. By the use of artificial light, we are able to see how the sun enters the tomb through the roof-box on the winter solstice. Watching the thin ray of light advance along the passage into the chamber, we can imagine how the Boyne people felt when the rays of the rising sun first entered the monument those winter mornings so long ago. Standing there, in the heart of the tomb, we feel a bond between us and our ancient ancestors who built this overwhelming place. We cannot share in the vision or world-view of those who brought this great monument into existence, however we can share in their pride in this magnificent and enduring achievement.

Newgrange is one of the most visited historical sites in Ireland, attracting visitors from all across the world.

ALSO BY LIAM MAC UISTIN

THE TÁIN
Illus. Donald Teskey

The most famous Irish legend of all in an exciting and easily-understood version. Tells of the great battle between the warrior Cúchulainn and his friend, Ferdia.

THE HUNT FOR DIARMAID AND GRÁINNE
Illus. Laura Cronin

A simple retelling of the great Celtic tale. Fionn loves Gráinne, but Gráinne loves the much younger Diarmaid – and runs off with him, setting in train a series of tragic and stirring events.

CELTIC MAGIC TALES
Illus. Maria A Negrin

The rich lore of magic from the ancient Celts fills these stories of the love quest of Mir and Aideen, the adventure of the sons of Tuireann, the mischievous Bricriu and the famous love epic of Deirdre.

OTHER BOOKS IN THE *EXPLORING* SERIES

EXPLORING THE BOOK OF KELLS
George Otto Simms
Illus. David Rooney

A beautiful and simple introduction to the Book of Kells. Here George Otto Simms, a world-renowned authority on the Book of Kells, reveals the mysteries hidden in this magnificent manuscript. He introduces the monks who made the book and guides the reader through the intricate detail of this ancient and exotic book.

EXPLORING THE WORLD OF COLMCILLE
Mairéad Ashe FitzGerald
Illus. Stephen Hall

A simple and accessible account of the life of this famous saint who founded the monastery at Iona. The book draws on history, art, literature and archaeology to tell the story of the saint and his times.

SAINT PATRICK
Ireland's Patron Saint
George Otto Simms
Illus. David Rooney

The unique life of Patrick as he wrote it in his Confession, and the legends surrounding him.

BRENDAN THE NAVIGATOR
George Otto Simms
Illus. David Rooney

Brendan's famous account of his voyages and the extraordinary imagery and unusual events of this ancient story, which was known all over the world in the Middle Ages.

THE VIKINGS IN IRELAND
Morgan Llywelyn

In Irish history the Vikings are often seen merely as attackers. This fascinating account gives the wider picture – how the Vikings significantly influenced Irish art and trade and the growth of towns and cities.

Send for our full-colour catalogue